AF438666

AN UNEXPECTED CONVERSATION

A Story-based Study of the
Woman at the Well

LIVING WATER

COLLECTIVE

This book is a spiritual reflection and study resource.

It is not intended as a substitute for professional counseling, medical care, or mental health treatment.

Readers are encouraged to seek appropriate support when needed.

An Unexpected Conversation – A Story-based study of the Woman at the Well
Written by **Gary A Collings**
Published by **Living Water Collective**

Contact: LivingWaterCollective2026@gmail.com

ISBN: 979-8-9949883-1-2

Printed in the United States of America.

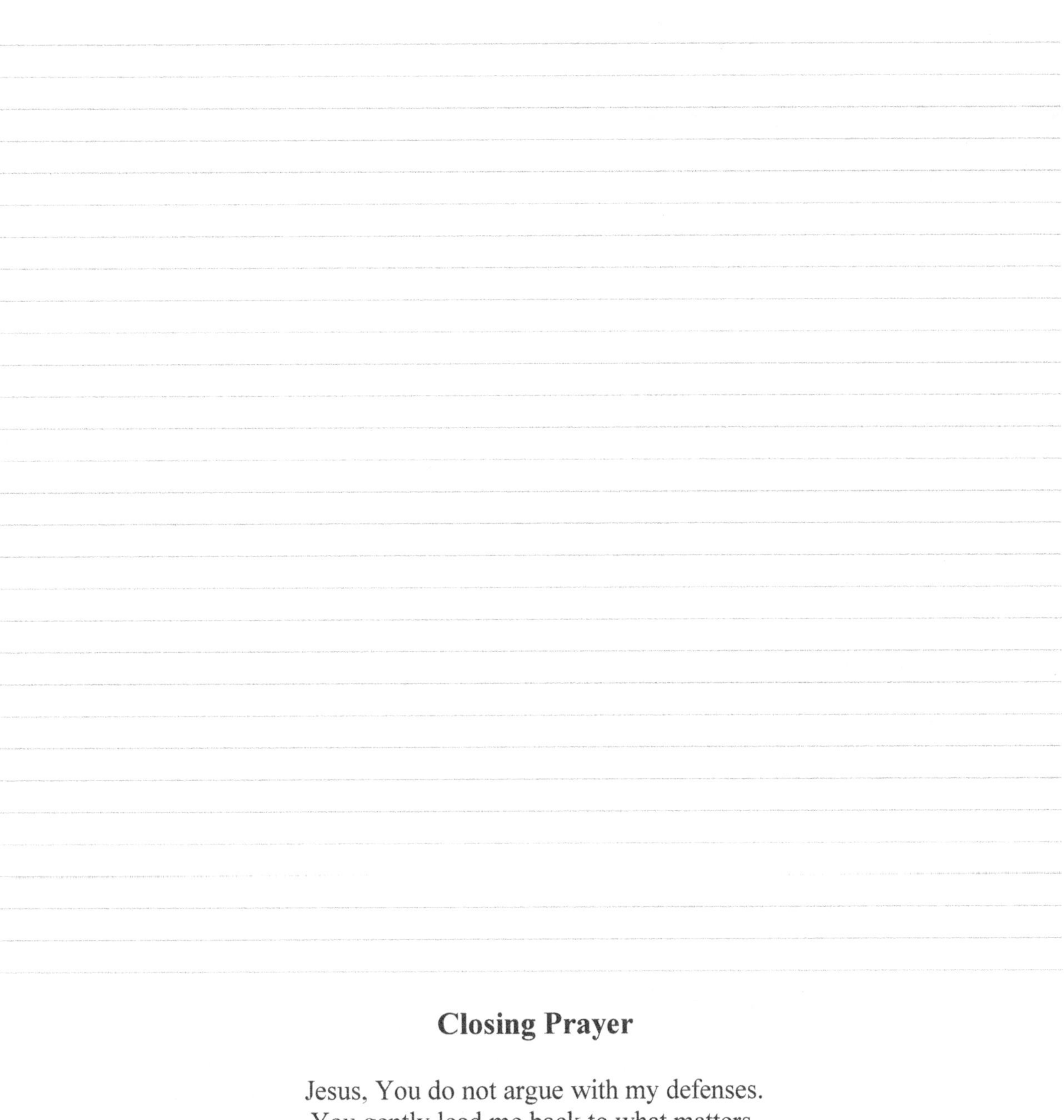

Closing Prayer

Jesus, You do not argue with my defenses.
You gently lead me back to what matters.
Teach me to worship You
in spirit and in truth.
Amen.

Leader / Reader Note

Jesus does not dismiss worship.
He re-centers it.

Worship here is not about *where* or *how* —
but about *who* we bring ourselves to
without hiding.

PART I — ENTERING THE STORY

Session 5 — Witness & Return

John 4:27–30, 39–42 (NIV)
When encounter becomes invitation

Purpose of This Session

To notice how encounter naturally moves outward,
not through obligation or certainty,
but through honesty and invitation.

This session is not about evangelism strategies.
It is about what happens
when living water begins to rise
and can no longer be contained.

Scripture Reading

(Read slowly. Either aloud or silently.)

John 4:27–30, 39–42 (NIV)

Just then His disciples returned and were surprised to find Him talking with a woman.
But no one asked, "What do You want?" or "Why are You talking with her?"

Then, leaving her water jar, the woman went back to the town and said to the people,
"Come, see a man who told me everything I ever did.
Could this be the Messiah?"

They came out of the town and made their way toward Him.

Many of the Samaritans from that town believed in Him because of the woman's testimony,
"He told me everything I ever did."

So when the Samaritans came to Him, they urged Him to stay with them, and He stayed two days.
And because of His words many more became believers.

They said to the woman,
"We no longer believe just because of what you said;
now we have heard for ourselves, and we know that this man really is the Savior of the world."

Reflections:

(Answer lightly. There is no need to explain.)

1. What stands out to you about **what the woman says** — and what she does not?

2. What do you notice about how belief spreads in this story?

Noticing the Moment

The woman does not return with answers.
She returns with honesty.

She does not claim certainty.
She asks a question.

She leaves her jar behind —
not because it no longer matters,
but because something else matters more.

Sit with this question:
What would it look like to invite others without needing to convince them?

Notes:

(You may write briefly or not at all.)

Where have you felt pressure to represent faith
instead of simply speaking from encounter?

Closing Prayer

Jesus, You do not ask me to persuade.
You ask me to witness.
Help me speak honestly
about what You have done in me
and trust You with the rest.
Amen.

Leader / Reader Note

Witness in this story is not performance.
It is overflow.
The woman is not the source of belief —
Jesus is.
Her role is simple:
Come and see.

From the Story to the Jars

You have walked with a woman back into her town.
You have listened as questions turned into truth,
and truth turned into witness.

Before anything is explained,
before anything is named,
notice this:

Jesus did not hand her a list.
He did not ask her to sort herself.
He did not rush her into clarity.

He simply stayed.

And in staying,
He allowed what she carried
to surface on its own.

What follows is not a sudden shift away from the story.
It is a way of staying with it.

Throughout John 4, the woman comes to the well carrying more than a water jar.
She carries longing.
Identity shaped by relationship.
Fear of being seen.
Religious language learned as protection.
Hope she barely trusts.

Jesus does not call these failures.
He does not label them sins to be fixed.
He treats them as places where thirst has learned how to survive.

In the pages ahead, we will use the image of **jars**
to name some of the common places people draw from
when life feels dry, heavy, uncertain, or exposed.

These jars are not diagnoses.
They are not labels.
They are not measures of spiritual maturity.

They are simply ways of noticing
where you may have learned to reach for water.

You are not being asked to choose a jar yet.
You are not being asked to evaluate yourself.

For now, read slowly.
Let language pass through without grabbing it.
Notice what feels familiar, and what doesn't.

Awareness comes before understanding.
Invitation comes before change.

Jesus never forced truth.
He invited it.

So will we.

Turn the page when you're ready.

The Twelve Jars — An Overview

(Read gently. No decisions required.)

The jars below describe **patterns**, not problems.
Most people recognize more than one.
Some jars appear only in certain seasons of life.

You are not meant to analyze yourself here.
Simply notice which descriptions feel recognizable — or quietly present.

Jar #1 — Unmet Longing

The thirst for something more
A quiet sense that life has not fully satisfied. Restlessness, ache, or hope held cautiously.

Jar #2 — Identity

The thirst to be known, chosen, and held
A tendency to understand yourself through roles, relationships, or how others respond to you.

Jar #3 — Religion & Performance

When doing for God replaces being with God
Faith experienced as effort, responsibility, or pressure more than rest and relationship.

Jar #4 — Knowledge & Control

The need to understand, manage, or stay ahead
Comfort found in clarity and certainty; unease when answers are missing.

Jar #5 — Fear & Shame

The fear of being exposed or failing
A habit of hiding parts of yourself to avoid judgment, disappointment, or rejection.

Jar #6 — Control & Self-Protection

Keeping life manageable and contained
Reliance on planning, independence, or guardedness to feel safe.

Jar #7 — Belonging & Witness

The desire to be included and understood
Longing to belong without having to edit your story or perform for acceptance.

Jar #8 — Approval & Validation

The hunger to be affirmed or appreciated
Encouragement feels life-giving; its absence can quietly drain you.

Jar #9 — Comparison & Secondhand Faith

Measuring your life by others' stories
Wondering whether your faith or life should look different by now.

Jar #10 — Hurry & Restlessness

The inability to slow down or rest
Staying busy to avoid what might surface in stillness.

Jar #11 — Loss & Letting Go

Grief, disappointment, or unresolved endings
Carrying quiet sorrow or guarded hope after something meaningful ended.

Jar #12 — Abiding & Wholeness

The invitation to remain, not strive
Not perfection, but a growing desire for steadiness, trust, and presence.

A Gentle Reminder

You may carry more than one jar.
You may carry different jars in different seasons.

Jesus meets you with every one of them.

On the next pages, you'll be invited to notice patterns more intentionally —
not to judge yourself,
but to listen more deeply.

There is no hurry.

The Surface Test

Noticing Where We Reach for Water

The Surface Test is not a test you pass or fail.
It is a tool for noticing.

These questions are designed to help you observe
the habits, reactions, and patterns
that shape your days, especially under stress, fatigue, or uncertainty.

You are not being asked to explain anything yet.
You are not being asked to diagnose yourself.
You are simply being invited to notice.

The places we instinctively reach for relief, reassurance, or control
often point toward deeper thirsts,
not to shame us,
but to guide us gently toward truth.

How to Take the Surface Test

• Read each statement slowly.
• Respond honestly, but lightly.
• There are no right or wrong answers.

Use the following scale:

1 — Not true for me
2 — Occasionally true
3 — Somewhat true
4 — Often true
5 — Very true

Answer based on your *usual patterns*,
not your best days or worst moments.

If a question feels insignificant, do not skip it.
Surface habits often point toward deeper places.

If a question feels uncomfortable, you may pause, or skip it.
Jesus never forced truth. He invited it.

As You Respond

• Do not try to interpret your answers yet.
• Do not total scores in your head.
• Do not compare yourself to others.

Simply notice:

- Which statements feel familiar
- Which sections stir recognition
- Which patterns repeat

Numbers are only markers.
Patterns are what matter.

A Gentle Reminder

This test does not tell you who you are.
It simply notices where you tend to draw water.

Some jars are learned through survival.
Some through habit.
Some through longing.

None of them disqualify you.

The Surface Test

Noticing What We Reach For

Answer each statement using the scale below.
Respond honestly, but lightly.

1 — Not true for me
2 — Occasionally true
3 — Somewhat true
4 — Often true
5 — Very true for me

There are no right or wrong answers.

Surface Test Statements

Daily Rhythms & Coping

(Often connected to restlessness, busyness, or escape)

1. I feel uneasy when my day has no clear structure or plan.
2. I reach for small comforts (food, caffeine, scrolling) when stressed.
3. I stay busy to avoid sitting with difficult thoughts.
4. Slowing down makes me feel restless or uncomfortable.

Relationships & Approval

(Often connected to approval, identity, or fear of disconnection)

5. I feel more secure when others need me.
6. I replay conversations, wondering how I came across.
7. I struggle when I feel overlooked or misunderstood.
8. I feel responsible for keeping relationships running smoothly.

Control & Certainty

(Often connected to knowledge, planning, or anxiety about the future)

9. I feel calmer when I know what's coming next.
10. Uncertainty makes me anxious, even about small things.
11. I prefer having answers rather than waiting.
12. I feel frustrated when plans change unexpectedly.

Faith & Performance

(Often connected to effort, comparison, or pressure)

13. I feel closer to God when I'm doing "well" spiritually.
14. I feel discouraged when my spiritual habits slip.
15. I compare my faith to others more than I'd like to admit.
16. I feel pressure to appear steady, even when I'm not.

Emotions & Inner Life

(Often connected to self-protection or avoidance)

17. I push through emotions rather than naming them.
18. I minimize my own struggles because others have it worse.
19. I feel uncomfortable admitting weakness.
20. I keep parts of my story private, even from God.

Image & Identity

(Often connected to worth, roles, or productivity)

21. I feel more confident when I'm productive or helpful.
22. I struggle when my role or usefulness is unclear.
23. I feel unsettled when I'm not sure who I am in a situation.
24. I feel defined by what I contribute.

Neutral / Unseen Questions

(Do not score — simply notice)

25. I enjoy routine more than spontaneity.
26. I find silence either refreshing or uncomfortable.
27. I tend to notice others' needs before my own.
28. I prefer depth over surface-level conversation.

Gentle Bridge Questions

(These prepare the heart for what comes next)

29. I sense there may be deeper reasons behind some of my habits.
30. I feel open to exploring what I carry beneath the surface.

Surface Test Reflection & Scoring Guide

Reading the Patterns — Not the Numbers

<u>Do not</u> add everything together.
There is no final score.

Instead, pause and notice.

Notice Resonance

Look back at your answers and gently mark:
• Any statements you rated **4 or 5**
• Any section where several statements stood out

Patterns matter more than numbers.

Name What Feels Familiar

Ask yourself (silently or in writing):

• Which sections felt most familiar?

• Which statements made you slow down?

• Which ones felt true without explanation?

You may notice more than one area.
That is normal.

Before the Jars

On the next pages, you will see twelve jars.

Each jar names a way people cope, strive, protect, or hope.
None of them are failures.
All of them are familiar.

You are not required to choose one.
You are not expected to recognize yourself fully in any of them.

Simply notice
which descriptions feel familiar,
which ones stir resistance,
or which ones feel quietly true.

Awareness is enough for now.

The Twelve Jars

Jar #1 — Unmet Longing

The quiet sense that something more is missing
You carry a persistent ache — for meaning, connection, or fulfillment — even when life appears "fine."

Jar #2 — Identity

The need to be known, chosen, or needed
Your sense of self has been shaped by roles, relationships, or how others respond to you.

Jar #3 — Religion & Performance

When doing for God replaces being with God
Faith feels effort-heavy. You strive to get it right, but rest feels distant.

Jar #4 — Knowledge & Control

The need to understand, manage, or stay ahead
You feel safest when things make sense. Uncertainty creates anxiety or restlessness.

Jar #5 — Fear & Shame

The fear of being exposed, failing, or disappointing
You guard parts of your story, unsure how they would be received if seen.

Jar #6 — Control & Self-Protection

Keeping life contained and manageable
You rely on planning, boundaries, or self-sufficiency to stay safe.

Jar #7 — Belonging & Witness

The desire to be included and understood
You long to belong without having to explain, perform, or prove yourself.

Jar #8 — Approval & Validation

The hunger to be affirmed or appreciated
Encouragement fuels you deeply — and its absence can quietly drain you.

Jar #9 — Comparison & Secondhand Faith

Measuring your life or faith by others' stories
You notice how others are doing — and sometimes wonder how you compare.

Jar #10 — Hurry & Restlessness

The inability to slow down or rest
Stillness feels uncomfortable. Activity becomes a refuge.

Jar #11 — Loss & Letting Go

Living with disappointment, grief, or unresolved endings
Something you hoped for or loved is gone — and the ache remains.

Jar #12 — Abiding & Wholeness

The desire to live from grace rather than striving
This jar reflects readiness, not arrival — a longing for steadiness and trust.

A Gentle Reminder

You may carry more than one jar.
Jars change with seasons.
Jesus does not shame the jar you carry —
He invites you to a better well.

How the Surface Test Connects to the Jars

The Surface Test is not designed to diagnose what is "wrong."
It helps you notice **where you instinctively reach for water**
when life feels pressured, uncertain, or emotionally full.

Each section of the test gently corresponds to one or more jars.
You do not need to figure this out as you answer —
this page simply helps you understand what the questions are noticing.

Patterns matter more than numbers.

Daily Rhythms & Coping

(Questions 1–4)
Often connected to **Jar #10 — Hurry & Restlessness**
and **Jar #1 — Unmet Longing**

These questions notice how you respond to stress, rest, and stillness.
Restlessness and constant motion often point to deeper thirsts —
not laziness or weakness.

Relationships & Approval

(Questions 5–8)
Often connected to **Jar #2 — Identity**
and **Jar #8 — Approval & Validation**

These questions explore how much security comes from being needed, affirmed, or relationally
steady.

Control & Certainty

(Questions 9–12)
Often connected to **Jar #4 — Knowledge & Control**
and **Jar #6 — Control & Self-Protection**

These questions notice how uncertainty affects you
and whether control has become a source of calm.

Faith & Performance

(Questions 13–16)
Often connected to **Jar #3 — Religion & Performance**
and sometimes **Jar #8 — Approval & Validation**

These questions gently surface whether faith feels like relationship
or responsibility — presence or pressure.

Emotions & Inner Life

(Questions 17–20)
Often connected to **Jar #5 — Fear & Shame**
and **Jar #11 — Loss & Letting Go**

These questions explore how you relate to vulnerability, weakness, and emotional honesty.

Image & Identity

(Questions 21–24)
Primarily connected to **Jar #2 — Identity**
and **Jar #9 — Comparison & Secondhand Faith**

These questions notice how much worth is drawn from usefulness, clarity of role, or comparison.

Neutral / Uneven Awareness Questions

(Questions 25–28)
These questions are **not scored**.
They help you notice personal tendencies that may interact with multiple jars.

Gentle Bridge Questions

(Questions 29–30)
These questions prepare you for the deeper work ahead.
If these resonate strongly, it may indicate readiness — not obligation — to continue.

A Pastoral Note

You may resonate with:

- One primary jar
- One secondary jar
- Or different jars in different seasons

This is normal.

The Surface Test does not tell you who you are.
It simply points toward **where your thirst has learned to go**.

The Deeper Test will explore *why*,
but only if and when you choose to continue.

Before You Continue

If you are here, you have already noticed something.
A pattern.
A pull.
A place that felt familiar.

There is no requirement to go further.
Many people stop after noticing, and that is enough.

The pages that follow are for those who feel a quiet invitation
to listen a little deeper,
not to fix what they find,
but to understand it with kindness.

Move slowly.
Pause often.
Answer only what you are ready to bring into the light.

Jesus never forced truth.
He invited it.

These questions explore not only *what* you reach for,
but *why* those places learned to hold water,
often shaped by pain, protection, loss, or survival.

The Deeper Test

Listening to the Bottom of the Jar

The Deeper Test is not a test you pass or fail.
It is not a measure of spiritual maturity.
It is not a tool for diagnosis or self-evaluation.

It is an invitation to listen more carefully.

Move slowly.
Pause often.
Answer only what you are ready to bring into the light.

Jesus never forced truth.
He invited it.

How to Take the Deeper Test

• Read each statement slowly.
• Respond honestly, but gently.
• You are not required to answer every question.
• Skipping a question is an act of wisdom, not avoidance.

Use the same scale as before:

1 — Not true for me
2 — Occasionally true
3 — Somewhat true
4 — Often true
5 — Very true

Answer based on your lived patterns,
not your best intentions or worst moments.

If a question feels overwhelming, pause.
If something stirs, breathe.
You do not need to resolve anything today.

As You Respond

• Do not rush to interpret your answers.
• Do not total everything.
• Do not compare yourself to anyone else.

Simply notice:

• Which questions slow you down
• Which ones stir emotion or resistance
• Which themes repeat quietly

Numbers are only markers.
Patterns are what matter.

A Word of Care

The Deeper Test explores tender places.
Some questions may touch experiences
that feel unresolved, painful, or vulnerable.

You are not expected to do this alone.

If at any point you feel overwhelmed:
• Pause
• Ground yourself
• Reach out to a trusted person
• Or bring what surfaced to God in prayer

This resource is not a substitute for counseling or care.
Slowing down is not failure.
It is often where healing begins.

A Gentle Reminder

This test does not tell you who you are.
It reveals where your thirst has learned to go.

Some jars formed through survival.
Some through habit.
Some through longing.

None of them disqualify you.

Living water does not flood the soul.
It rises, patiently.

The Deeper Test

Listening to What Lives Beneath the Jar

Before you begin, pause.

This is not a test you must finish.
It is not a measure of spiritual maturity.
It is not a diagnosis.

The questions that follow explore places shaped by experience, protection, loss, and survival.
Some questions may feel familiar.
Others may feel tender.
Some may not feel relevant at all.

You are not required to answer everything.
You are free to skip any question.
You may stop at any point.

Jesus never forced truth.
He invited it.

Use the same scale as before:

1 — Not true for me
2 — Occasionally true
3 — Somewhat true
4 — Often true
5 — Very true for me

Answer based on what feels *generally true*, not what you wish were true.

Move slowly.
Pause when needed.
Truth does not expire.

Deeper Test Statements

Control & Self-Protection

(Often connected to safety, planning, and guardedness)

1. I feel anxious when I cannot control outcomes.
2. I rely on planning or preparation to feel safe.
3. Letting go feels risky, even with God.
4. I struggle to trust when the future feels unclear.

Identity & Worth

(Often connected to roles, usefulness, and being needed)

5. I feel unsure of my value when I am not needed.
6. I define myself by roles I play or responsibilities I carry.
7. I fear being replaceable or forgotten.
8. I struggle to believe I am loved apart from what I do.

Fear, Shame & Exposure

(Often connected to hiding, silence, or self-protection)

9. I avoid situations where my weaknesses might be seen.
10. I carry shame about parts of my story I rarely name.
11. I fear how others would see me if they knew everything.
12. I keep emotional distance to protect myself.

Relationships & Attachment

(Often connected to belonging, loss, or fear of abandonment)

13. I fear being left more than I admit.
14. I stay in unhealthy patterns to avoid being alone.
15. I adjust who I am to keep peace in relationships.
16. I struggle to believe others will stay when I'm honest.

Faith, Religion & Performance

(Often connected to effort, guilt, or spiritual pressure)

17. I feel pressure to appear spiritually steady.
18. I feel guilty when my faith feels quiet or weak.
19. I use spiritual activity to avoid deeper pain.
20. I fear disappointing God.

Comfort, Escape & Coping

(Often connected to numbing, relief, or avoidance)

21. I turn to habits or distractions to numb difficult feelings.
22. I rely on temporary relief rather than lasting healing.
23. I struggle to sit with pain without escaping it.
24. I avoid emotional discomfort whenever possible.

Busyness & Avoidance

(Often connected to restlessness and fear of stillness)

25. I stay busy to avoid slowing down.
26. Silence makes me uncomfortable.
27. I feel restless when life becomes quiet.
28. I avoid rest because it feels unsafe or unproductive.

Trust & Surrender

(Often connected to control, fear, or delayed trust)

29. I find it hard to believe God is enough for me.
30. I struggle to receive rather than earn.
31. I fear what surrender might require of me.
32. I hesitate to bring my full truth to God.

Listening Questions – (these questions are not scored)

(Do not score — simply notice)

33. I sense God gently drawing my attention to something specific.

A Gentle Word Before You Begin

Before you turn the page, pause.

This is **not therapy**.
It is not designed to diagnose, treat, or resolve what you carry.
It is a place to notice and listen.

This is **not a test you must pass**.
There are no right answers.
There is no score that defines you.

You are not being measured.
You are being invited.

And **honesty matters more than completion**.
You do not need to answer every question.
You do not need to move quickly.

You are free to skip what feels premature.

Jesus never forced truth.
He invited it.

So take your time.
Answer lightly or honestly, both are faithful.
And trust that even what you do not yet name
is already known by God.

How to Use This Workbook

This workbook is not meant to be rushed.
It is designed to be **entered gently**, used **honestly**, and returned to as needed.

You are not required to complete every page.
You are not expected to "fix" anything.
This is a place to notice, listen, and respond at your own pace.

Individual Use

This workbook may be used on your own.

• Read slowly
• Pause when something stirs
• Write only what feels honest
• Skip questions that feel premature

Some people will move quickly through the story and linger in the reflection.
Others will return to the same jar repeatedly over time.

Both are faithful ways of engaging.

Couples Use

This workbook may be used by couples **side-by-side**, not face-to-face.

Each person should:
• Read individually
• Complete reflections privately
• Take the Surface and Deeper Tests separately

When sharing, focus on **patterns**, not explanations.
You are not required to share scores or details.

Try language like:
• "This jar felt familiar."
• "This question stayed with me."
• "I'm noticing where I reach for control."

Avoid:
• Fixing
• Interpreting
• Explaining your partner's responses

Your goal is not agreement.
Your goal is awareness and presence.

Group Use

This workbook may be used in small groups, retreats, or guided settings.

Best practices:
• Groups of 6–10 people
• Individual reflection before group discussion
• Sharing at the pattern level, not the story level
• Passing is always allowed

Leaders should create space, not conclusions.
This is not a counseling curriculum.
It is a guided listening experience.

Permission to Go Slowly

You are allowed to:
• Stop mid-page
• Return later
• Sit with a question for days or weeks
• Leave a jar unnamed for now

Jesus never rushed truth.
He invited it.

If a section feels tender, pause.
If a question feels heavy, set it down.
If something surfaces that feels overwhelming, reach out to a trusted person.

Living water does not flood the soul.
It rises patiently.

PART I — ENTERING THE STORY

Session 1 — Meeting at the Well -

John 4:1–9 (NIV)
Jesus initiates the conversation

Purpose of This Session

To ground participants in the biblical story **without over-teaching**,
and to invite quiet awareness before any analysis, jars, or tests appear.

This session is about **arrival**, not insight.

Scripture Reading

(Read slowly. Either aloud or silently.)

John 4:1–9 (NIV)

Now Jesus learned that the Pharisees had heard that he was gaining
and baptizing more disciples than John,
although in fact it was not Jesus who baptized, but his disciples.

So he left Judea and went back once more to Galilee.

Now he had to go through Samaria.

So he came to a town in Samaria called Sychar, near the plot of
ground Jacob had given to his son Joseph.

Jacob's well was there, and Jesus, tired as he was from the journey, sat down by the well.
It was about noon.

When a Samaritan woman came to draw water, Jesus said to her,
"Will you give me a drink?"
(His disciples had gone into the town to buy food.)

The Samaritan woman said to him,
"You are a Jew and I am a Samaritan woman. How can you ask me for a drink?"
(For Jews do not associate with Samaritans.)

Reflections:

(Do not rush. Answer lightly.)

1. **What stands out to you this time as you read this scene?**
   (A phrase, a detail, a feeling, not an explanation.)

2. **What feels uncomfortable, surprising, or familiar about this encounter?**

Noticing the Scene

- Jesus is tired.
- The woman arrives alone.
- The conversation begins with a simple request.

Sit with this question:

What do you notice about how Jesus meets her, before anything is asked of her?

Notes:

(There is no right length.)

What does this opening scene stir in you, if anything?

Closing Prayer

Leader / Reader Note

You do not need to understand everything yet.
You do not need to see yourself clearly yet.
This session is simply about **showing up**.

PART I — ENTERING THE STORY

Session 2 — Living Water

John 4:10–15 (NIV)
Jesus names a deeper thirst

Purpose of This Session

To listen to what Jesus offers **before** He addresses truth, history, or change,
and to notice how desire begins to surface.

This session is about **thirst**, not solutions.

Scripture Reading

(Read slowly. Either aloud or silently.)

John 4:10–15 (NIV)

Jesus answered her,
**"If you knew the gift of God and who it is that asks you for a drink,
you would have asked him and he would have given you living water."**

"Sir," the woman said, "you have nothing to draw with and the well is deep.
Where can you get this living water?
Are you greater than our father Jacob, who gave us the well and drank from it himself,
as did also his sons and his livestock?"

Jesus answered,
**"Everyone who drinks this water will be thirsty again,
but whoever drinks the water I give them will never thirst.
Indeed, the water I give them will become in them a spring of water
welling up to eternal life."**

The woman said to him,
**"Sir, give me this water so that I won't get thirsty
and have to keep coming here to draw water."**

Reflections:

(Answer lightly. There is no need to explain.)

1. **What words or phrases lingered as you read this exchange?**

2. **What do you notice about what the woman is hoping this "living water" will change?**

Noticing the Conversation

Jesus speaks of **living water**.
The woman speaks of **relief from returning**.

Sit with this question:

What kind of thirst do you hear in her response, practical, emotional, spiritual, or something else?

Notes:

(You may write briefly or not at all.)

Where do you notice yourself hoping that something, anything,
will make life feel lighter, easier, or less demanding?

Closing Prayer

Jesus, You know my thirst
even when I don't have words for it.
Help me listen before I try to fix it.
Amen.

Leader / Reader Note

The woman has not yet been asked for truth.
She has not been corrected or instructed.
She has only been **invited to want something more.**

PART I — ENTERING THE STORY

Session 3 — Truth & Identity

John 4:16–18 (NIV)
Jesus names what has shaped her thirst

Purpose of This Session

To notice how Jesus speaks truth **without accusation,**
and how identity often forms around what we reach for to feel chosen, secure, or known.

This session is not about confession.
It is about **recognition.**

Scripture Reading

(Read slowly. Either aloud or silently.)

John 4:16–18 (NIV)

He told her, **"Go, call your husband and come back."**

"I have no husband," she replied.

Jesus said to her,
**"You are right when you say you have no husband.
The fact is, you have had five husbands,
and the man you now have is not your husband.
What you have just said is quite true."**

Reflections:

(Answer lightly. There is no need to explain.)

1. **What do you notice about how Jesus brings truth into the conversation?**

2. **What stands out to you about what He names, and what He does not?**

Noticing the Moment

Jesus does not ask for the woman's past.
He asks for her **present**.

Sit with this question:

Why do you think Jesus begins with "Go, call your husband" instead of naming her history first?

Notes:

(You may write briefly or not at all.)

Where have relationships, roles, or being chosen
quietly shaped how you see yourself?

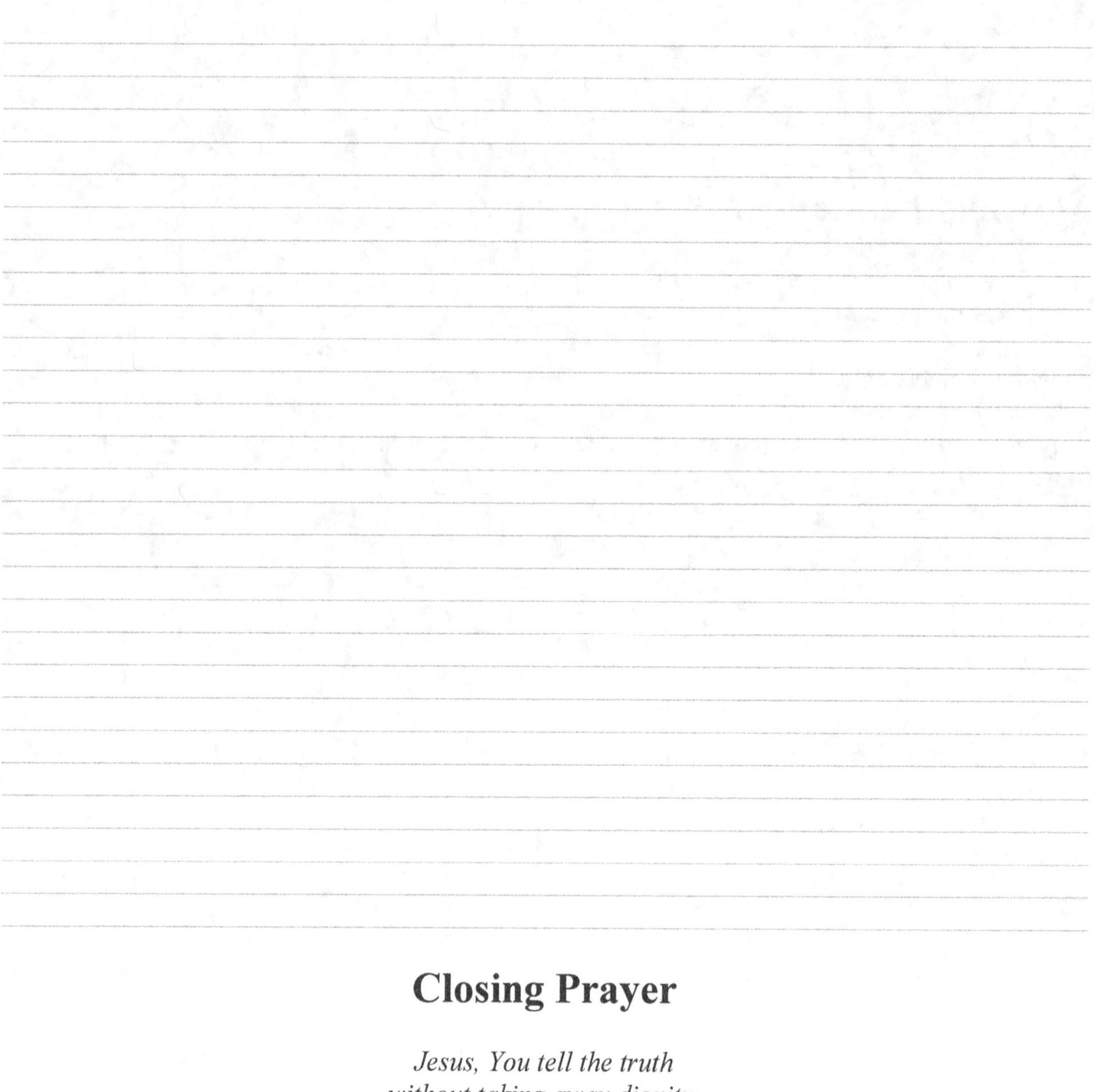

Closing Prayer

*Jesus, You tell the truth
without taking away dignity.
Help me trust You
with what has shaped me.*
Amen.

Leader / Reader Note:

Jesus does not reduce her to her history.
He names it — and then stays.
Truth here is not exposure.
It is invitation.

PART I — ENTERING THE STORY

Session 4 — Worship & Deflection

John 4:19–24 (NIV)
When theology becomes a refuge

Purpose of This Session

To notice how we sometimes shift into **religious language**
when truth feels too close,
and how Jesus gently redirects worship
from place and performance
to presence and truth.

This session is not about getting worship "right."
It is about **where we hide when truth feels exposed**.

Scripture Reading

(Read slowly. Either aloud or silently.)

John 4:19–24 (NIV)
The woman said, "Sir, I can see that you are a prophet.
Our ancestors worshiped on this mountain,
but you Jews claim that the place where we must worship is in Jerusalem."

Jesus replied,
"Woman, Believe me, a time is coming when you will worship the Father
neither on this mountain nor in Jerusalem.
You Samaritans worship what you do not know;
we worship what we do know, for salvation is from the Jews.
Yet a time is coming and has now come when the true worshippers will worship the Father in the
Spirit and in truth, for they are the kind of worshippers the Father seeks.

God is spirit, and his worshippers must worship in the Spirit and in truth"

Reflections:

(Answer lightly. There is no need to explain.)

1. When the conversation turns to worship, what do you notice happening in the woman's response?

2. Where do you notice Jesus redirecting the focus of the conversation?

Noticing the Moment

The woman does not deny what Jesus has said about her life.
But she shifts the conversation to something safer,
a long-standing religious debate.

This is not rebellion.
It is protection.

Sit with this question:
When truth feels close, where do you tend to redirect the conversation?

Notes:

(You may write briefly or not at all.)

Where has faith become something you explain, debate, or perform
instead of a place where you are known?

34. I feel both resistance and longing as I answer these questions.
35. I recognize patterns that have shaped how I survive.
36. I feel invited — not forced — to respond.

A Gentle Pause

If something surfaced as you answered, do not rush to fix it.

Sit with it.
Name it.
Bring it to Jesus.

You may stop here.
You may continue later.
You may never return to some questions.

Living water does not flood the soul.
It rises patiently.

Before Scoring

You are not required to score this test.

Scoring is a tool for noticing patterns,
not a requirement for growth.

If you choose to continue, the next pages will help you gently identify
which jars may be most present **right now**.

There is no "best" jar.
There is no "worst" jar.

Each jar simply reveals
where Jesus may be inviting you
to drink more deeply.

Deeper Test Results

Listening to Where the Water Has Been Drawn

You may have noticed one jar rise more clearly than others.
You may have noticed more than one.
You may still feel unsure.

There is no rush.

These pages are not explanations.
They are reflections.

Each jar names a place where thirst learned how to survive,
not a flaw to correct,
not a label to carry.

Read only the page that matches what stood out most.
You can return to the others later, or not at all.

Living water does not demand speed.
It invites honesty.

Interpreting the Deeper Test

Do **not** total your score.

Instead, notice:

- Which questions stirred emotion
- Which themes repeated
- Which jars feel familiar rather than surprising

These patterns are **not failures**.
They are places where God may already be at work.

If you want clearer direction, the next page helps you summarize.

If you need to pause here, do so.
Scoring can wait.
Truth does not expire.

STEP 1: Transfer Your Scores

After completing the Deeper Test, copy your score for each question into the space below.

Use the same scale you used in the test:
1 = Not at all true
2 = Rarely true
3 = Sometimes true
4 = Often true
5 = Very true

STEP 2: Add Your Jar Scores

For each Jar, **add the numbers** listed next to it.
Write the **total** in the shaded box.

      ✱ You do not need to average unless you want to. Totals work just fine.

Jar #1 — Unmet Longing

(Questions 21, 22, 23, 24, 33, 34,35,36)

21 ___
22 ___
23 ___
24 ___
33 ___
34 ___
35 ___
36 ___

TOTAL: ____   **PAGE 53**

Jar #2 — Identity

(Questions 5, 6, 7, 8, 13, 14,15,16)

5 ___
6 ___
7 ___
8 ___
13 ___
14 ___
15 ___
16 ___

TOTAL: ____   **PAGE 54**

Jar #3 — Religion & Performance

(Questions 17, 18, 19, 20)

17 ___
18 ___
19 ___
20 ___

TOTAL: ____   **PAGE 55**

Jar #4 — Knowledge & Control

(Questions 1, 2, 3, 4, 29, 30,31,32)

1 ___
2 ___
3 ___
4 ___
29 ___
30 ___
31 ___
32 ___

TOTAL: ____   **PAGE 56**

Jar #5 — Fear & Shame

(Questions 9, 10, 11, 12)

9 ___
10 ___
11 ___
12 ___

TOTAL: ____   **PAGE 57**

Jar #6 — Control & Self-Protection

(Questions 1, 2, 3, 4, 25, 26, 27, 28)

1 ___
2 ___
3 ___
4 ___
25 ___
26 ___
27 ___
28 ___

TOTAL: ____   **PAGE 58**

Jar #7 — Belonging & Witness

(Questions 13, 14, 15, 16, 33, 34, 35, 36)

13 ___
14 ___
15 ___
16 ___
33 ___
34 ___
35 ___
36 ___

TOTAL: ____   **PAGE 59**

Jar #8 — Approval & Validation

(Questions 5, 6, 7, 8, 17, 18, 19, 20)

5 ____
6 ____
7 ____
8 ____
17 ____
18 ____
19 ____
20 ____

TOTAL: ____   **PAGE 60**

Jar #9 — Comparison & Secondhand Faith

(Questions 15, 18, 33, 34, 35, 36)

15 ____
18 ____
33 ____
34 ____
35 ____
36 ____

TOTAL: ____   **PAGE 61**

Jar #10 — Hurry & Restlessness

(Questions 25, 26, 27, 28)

25 ____
26 ____
27 ____
28 ____

TOTAL: ____   **PAGE 62**

Jar #11 — Loss & Letting Go

(Questions 9, 10, 11, 12, 29, 30, 31, 32)

9 ___
10 ___
11 ___
12 ___
29 ___
30 ___
31 ___
32 ___

TOTAL: ____ **PAGE 63**

Jar #12 — Abiding & Wholeness

(Questions 33, 34, 35, 36)

33 ___
34 ___
35 ___
36 ___

TOTAL: ____ **PAGE 64**

Identify Your Primary Jar

- Circle the **highest total**
- That is your **Primary Jar**
- If a second jar is close, note it, many people carry more than one

✱ There is no "best" or "worst" jar.
Each jar simply reveals where Jesus may be inviting you to drink more deeply.

A Jesus Reminder

This test does not tell you who you are.
It reveals where you have been drawing water.

Jesus never shamed the woman for her jar.
He invited her to leave it behind.

Next Step

Turn to the ***Jar Reflection Page*** that matches your highest score.
Read slowly.
Pray honestly.
And remember:

"The water I give will become a spring within you."

Living Water Collective

The Twelve Jars — A Visual Summary

These jars are not labels.
They are places where thirst has learned to draw water.
Jesus does not shame the jar you carry, He invites you to a better well.

****These pages reflect where your scores fell, not who you are.***

Jar #1 — Unmet Longing

When desire quietly becomes ache

You carry a longing that has not disappeared with time.
It may show up as restlessness, quiet dissatisfaction, or hope held cautiously.
Life may look "fine," yet something still feels unfinished.

Jesus does not shame longing.
He follows it.

Unmet desire is not a failure of faith.
It is often the place where God is inviting you to receive rather than strive.

Invitation
What longing have you learned to manage instead of bringing to Jesus?

Prayer
Jesus, You see what I want but rarely name.
Meet me where longing still lives.
Teach me to receive, not reach.
Amen.

Notes & Reflections:

Jar #2 — Identity

When worth is shaped by roles or relationships

You may feel steady when you are needed —
and unsettled when you are not.
Your sense of self may have formed quietly through relationships, approval, or responsibility.

Jesus sees you apart from what you do.
He does not define you by who stayed or who left.

Identity becomes heavy when it is earned.
Living water restores identity as something received.

Invitation
What would change if Jesus — not your past — named you?

Prayer
Jesus, help me loosen what I use to define myself.
Teach me who I am in You.
Let me rest there.
Amen.

Notes & Reflections:

Jar #3 — Religion & Performance

When doing for God replaces being with God

You may be faithful, sincere, and committed —
yet quietly tired.
Spiritual activity may have become effort more than encounter.

Jesus does not dismantle worship.
He deepens it.

Living water invites you out of performance
and back into presence.

Invitation
Where might faith have become something you manage rather than receive?

Prayer
Jesus, I bring You my effort and my exhaustion.
Teach me how to be with You again.
Amen.

Notes & Reflections:

Jar #4 — Knowledge & Control

When understanding delays trust

Clarity brings comfort.
Answers feel safer than waiting.
Uncertainty may create restlessness or quiet anxiety.

Jesus does not oppose understanding —
but He will not be postponed by it.

Living water begins where certainty ends.

Invitation
What answer are you waiting for before trusting more fully?

Prayer
Jesus, help me trust You where I want clarity.
Teach me to stay present in the unknown.
Amen.

Notes & Reflections:

Jar #5 — Fear & Shame

When hiding feels safer than healing

You may guard parts of your story,
unsure how they would be received if seen.
Silence may have felt protective — even necessary.

Jesus does not expose you to humiliation.
He reveals you to freedom.

Living water moves at the pace of safety.

Invitation
What fear has shaped where you stay silent?

Prayer
Jesus, meet me gently where I hide.
Teach me that light can be kind.
Amen.

Notes & Reflections:

Jar #6 — Control & Self-Protection

When survival strategies linger

Planning, self-sufficiency, or guardedness may have once kept you safe.
What helped you survive may now be limiting your freedom.

Jesus does not take the jar from your hands.
He waits until you are ready to loosen your grip.

Invitation
What are you afraid would happen if you let go — even a little?

Prayer
Jesus, help me trust without rushing.
Teach me what safety looks like with You.
Amen.

Notes & Reflections:

Jar #7 — Belonging & Witness

When fear questions your credibility

You may hesitate to speak honestly,
believing your story disqualifies you.

Jesus entrusted His name to someone still becoming whole.

Living water turns testimony into invitation — not perfection.

Invitation
Who might need your honesty more than your certainty?

Prayer
Jesus, help me speak from encounter, not image.
Use what You have already done.
Amen.

Notes & Reflections:

Jar #8 — Approval & Validation

When affirmation feels essential

Encouragement strengthens you deeply.
Its absence may quietly drain you.

Jesus does not anchor truth to consensus.
Living water roots faith deeper than applause.

Invitation
Where have you looked to others to confirm what God has already spoken?

Prayer
Jesus, help me listen for Your voice above all others.
Anchor me there.
Amen.

Notes & Reflections:

Jar #9 — Comparison & Secondhand Faith

When belief borrows confidence

Your faith may have begun through others —
and comparison may have crept in quietly.

Jesus does not ask you to replicate another story.
He invites personal encounter.

Invitation
What would it look like to trust your own experience with Jesus?

Prayer
Jesus, meet me personally.
Help me walk my own path with You.
Amen.

Notes & Reflections:

Jar #10 — Hurry & Restlessness

When stillness feels unsafe

Movement may feel necessary.
Slowing down may feel uncomfortable or even threatening.

Jesus stayed.
Living water works patiently — reshaping through presence.

Invitation
What might surface if you allowed Jesus to linger?

Prayer
Jesus, teach me how to rest without fear.
Stay with me here.
Amen.

Notes & Reflections:

Jar #11 — Loss & Letting Go

When guarding joy feels wise

Loss may have taught you to brace for disappointment.
Hope may feel fragile.

Jesus leaves — but the water remains.

Living water teaches trust beyond proximity.

Invitation
Where have you guarded joy out of fear it will be taken?

Prayer
Jesus, help me trust what You have given will endure.
Teach me how to hope again.
Amen.

Notes & Reflections:

Jar #12 — Abiding & Wholeness

When readiness quietly appears

This jar does not mean arrival.
It reflects a growing desire to live from grace rather than striving.

Wholeness is not the absence of need.
It is the presence of trust.

Invitation
What would it look like to live from what has already been given?

Prayer
Jesus, help me remain with You.
Teach me how to live from the water.
Amen.

Notes & Reflections:

Final Pastoral Reminder

No jar defines you.
Each one simply marks a place where Jesus is already at work.

Living water does not rush.
It rises.

A Gentle Release

You do not have to finish this workbook to be faithful.

You do not have to answer every question,
name every jar,
or understand everything that surfaced.

Some people will move through these pages quickly.
Others will pause often, linger, or set the book down for a while.
Some will return later.
Some may not.

All of these are faithful responses.

What matters is not how much you completed,
but that you noticed, even briefly,
where you tend to reach for water.

If a jar felt familiar,
you are not alone.

If a question stayed with you,
you are not behind.

If something surfaced that feels unfinished,
you are not failing.

Jesus did not rush the woman at the well.
He did not follow her home to monitor progress.
He stayed long enough for truth to rise,
and trusted what would happen next.

You are free to close this book now.

You are free to return later.

You are free to carry what you noticed
without needing to fix it.

Living water does not demand completion.
It invites trust.

May what you discovered remain gentle,
may what felt heavy become lighter with time,
and may you remember this:

You are not late.
You are not overlooked.
You are not disqualified by what you carry.

The One who met a woman at a well
still meets people patiently,
not with pressure,
but with presence.

Rest here.

Drink when you are ready.

And live from the water
that does not run dry.

Amen.

Appendix A — How the Jars Are Mapped

(For leaders, facilitators, and curious readers)

This appendix explains how the reflection questions and tests in this workbook connect to the twelve jars.

You do **not** need this section to benefit from the workbook.
Many readers will skip it entirely — and that is appropriate.

This section exists to provide transparency and clarity
for leaders, facilitators, counselors, and those who want to understand the structure behind the questions.

What the Jars Represent

The jars are **not diagnoses**.
They are **not personality types**.
They are **not spiritual rankings**.

Each jar names a **common human pattern** — a place where people often learn to draw relief, reassurance, control, or meaning when life feels uncertain, painful, or demanding.

In John 4, Jesus never labels the woman.
He notices where she has been drawing water —
and invites her to a different source.

The jars follow the same posture.

How the Questions Were Designed

The workbook includes two kinds of reflection tools:

- **The Surface Test** — notices *what* patterns show up
- **The Deeper Test** — explores *why* those patterns may exist

Each section of questions corresponds to one or more jars.
Some jars draw from **multiple question sets** — this is intentional.

Human lives are layered.
Patterns overlap.
Healing rarely happens in straight lines.

Important Use-With-Care Note

- A **high score does not mean something is "wrong."**
- A **low score does not mean a jar is absent.**
- Scores can shift with stress, season, or life events.

Jars describe **where thirst has learned to go,**
not who a person is.

Deeper Test → Jar Mapping

Jar #1 — Unmet Longing

Primary Question Sets:
• Comfort, Escape & Coping (21–24)
• Listening Questions (33–36)

Why:
Longing often appears indirectly — through restlessness, numbing, or quiet ache rather than direct language.

John 4 Anchor:
"Sir, give me this water…"

Jar #2 — Identity

Primary Question Sets:
• Identity & Worth (5–8)
• Relationships & Attachment (13–16)

Why:
Identity frequently forms through belonging, roles, and fear of being unchosen.

John 4 Anchor:
"You have had five husbands…"

Jar #3 — Religion & Performance

Primary Question Sets:
• Faith, Religion & Performance (17–20)

Why:
These questions isolate effort-driven faith without shaming sincerity.

John 4 Anchor:
"Our ancestors worshiped on this mountain…"

Jar #4 — Knowledge & Control

Primary Question Sets:
• Control & Self-Protection (1–4)
• Trust & Surrender (29–32)

Why:
Control often hides behind preparation, clarity, and waiting for answers.

John 4 Anchor:
"When Messiah comes, He will explain everything…"

Jar #5 — Fear & Shame

Primary Question Sets:
• Fear, Shame & Exposure (9–12)

Why:
This jar requires clear boundaries — no overlap — to avoid emotional overload.

John 4 Anchor:
The disciples returning and seeing her.

Jar #6 — Control & Self-Protection

Primary Question Sets:
• Control & Self-Protection (1–4)
• Busyness & Avoidance (25–28)

Why:
Survival strategies evolve — planning, control, and busyness often protect the same wound.

John 4 Anchor:
Leaving the jar behind.

Jar #7 — Belonging & Witness

Primary Question Sets:
• Relationships & Attachment (13–16)
• Listening Questions (33–36)

Why:
Witness emerges where fear of rejection meets longing to belong.

John 4 Anchor:
"Come and see…"

Jar #8 — Approval & Validation

Primary Question Sets:
• Identity & Worth (5–8)
• Faith, Religion & Performance (17–20)

Why:
Approval sits between identity and faith — worth measured externally.

John 4 Anchor:
Many believed because of her testimony.

Jar #9 — Comparison & Secondhand Faith

Primary Question Sets:
• Faith & Performance (15, 18)
• Listening Questions (33–36)

Why:
This jar appears when belief relies on others' certainty rather than personal encounter.

John 4 Anchor:
"We no longer believe just because of what you said…"

Jar #10 — Hurry & Restlessness

Primary Question Sets:
• Busyness & Avoidance (25–28)

Why:
Stillness avoidance is its own signal and does not need overlap.

John 4 Anchor:
Jesus stayed two days.

Jar #11 — Loss & Letting Go

Primary Question Sets:
• Trust & Surrender (29–32)
• Fear & Shame (9–12)

Why:
Loss often reshapes trust and vulnerability after healing has begun.

John 4 Anchor:
Jesus leaving, but the water remaining.

Jar #12 — Abiding & Wholeness

Primary Question Sets:
• Listening Questions (33–36)
• Balanced resonance across multiple jars

Why:
This jar reflects integration, not perfection, readiness rather than arrival.

John 4 Anchor:
Living from the water.

A Final Word for Leaders

Do not assign jars.
Do not interpret scores for others.
Do not rush insight.

Your role is to **hold space**, not conclusions.

Jesus did not analyze the woman.
He stayed.

Do the same.

How the Book and Workbook Are Meant to Be Used

A brief guide for reviewers

These two resources are designed to work together, but they serve **different purposes** and can also stand alone.

The Book

An Unexpected Conversation
Primary posture: receiving

The book is a **story-based, reflective journey** through John 4.
It is meant to be *read*, not worked through.

How it functions:

- Invites the reader into the biblical story emotionally and imaginatively
- Low-demand, non-intrusive, and safe for a wide audience
- Can be read privately, devotionally, or discussed lightly in a group
- Allows people to recognize themselves *without being asked to name anything yet*

Best use cases:

- Personal reading
- Introductory small groups
- Pastoral gifting or recommendation
- Readers who are not ready for structured reflection
- A first step before deeper work

The book's role is to **open the door** and create trust.

The Workbook

An Unexpected Conversation — Workbook
Primary posture: noticing and responding

The workbook is a **guided listening experience** that follows the same story but slows the reader down.

How it functions:

- Moves from story → awareness → pattern noticing
- Uses reflection, journaling, and the jar framework to name habits gently
- Invites honesty without pressure to disclose or "fix" anything
- Designed to be used selectively — not every page must be completed

Best use cases:

- Retreats (weekend or half-day formats)
- Small groups with clear facilitation
- Couples (side-by-side, not face-to-face processing)
- Individuals who sense readiness for deeper reflection

The workbook's role is to **hold space** once trust has been established.

How They Work Together

- The **book builds safety**
- The **workbook builds awareness**
- The book invites recognition
- The workbook invites response

Someone can benefit from either one on its own.
But when used together, the journey feels more complete.

A Word About Pace

Neither resource is meant to be rushed.

- The book can be read in a few sittings
- The workbook may take weeks—or return seasons later
- Slowness is not failure; it is part of the design

The goal is not completion.
The goal is **gentle encounter**.

Retreat Schedule Handout

An Unexpected Conversation

Weekend Retreat Schedule

This retreat is not about finishing a workbook.
It is about creating space to notice, listen, and be gently invited.

You are free to participate at your own pace.
Passing is always allowed.

Friday Evening — Arrival at the Well

Focus: Safety, story, and grounding
No tests. No pressure. Just arrival.

- Welcome & posture setting
- Session 1: *Meeting at the Well* (John 4:1–9)
- Session 2: *Living Water* (John 4:10–15)
- Quiet reflection or prayer

Goal: To feel safe, not exposed.

Saturday Morning — Recognition

Focus: Truth without accusation

- Session 3: *Truth & Identity* (John 4:16–18)
- Session 4: *Worship & Deflection* (John 4:19–24)
- Pattern-level reflection (optional sharing)

Goal: Awareness, not explanation.

Saturday Afternoon — Naming Patterns

Focus: Noticing without diagnosing

- Session 5: *Witness & Return* (John 4:27–30, 39–42)
- Introduction to the Twelve Jars
- Surface Test (taken privately)

Important: Nothing you notice today needs to be fixed before you leave.

Sunday Morning — Release & Sending

Focus: Presence, not pressure

- Scripture reflection (John 4:13–14)
- Prayer or communion
- Closing blessing

Leader Guardrails for a Weekend Intensive

(For facilitators — this protects the room)

Leader Guardrails — Please Read First

This retreat is a **guided listening experience**, not a counseling event.

Your role is to:

- Hold space
- Slow the pace
- Protect safety
- Keep Jesus centered

Not to:

- Interpret responses
- Assign jars
- Fix patterns
- Push disclosure

Essential Guardrails

1. Pace Over Progress
Do not try to "finish" material.
Stopping early is success.

2. Patterns, Not Stories
Invite language like:

- "I noticed…"
- "This felt familiar…"
- "I'm becoming aware…"

Discourage:

- Detailed personal histories
- Cross-talk or advice
- Spiritual explanations of someone clse's experience

3. No Public Scoring

- Surface Test scores are private
- No one shares numbers
- Leaders never interpret results

4. Normalize Pausing

If emotion surfaces:

- Pause
- Lower your voice
- Breathe together
- Say:
  "Thank you for trusting the space. Let's slow down."

5. Deeper Test Is Optional

The Deeper Test is:

- Not assigned during the weekend
- Not discussed publicly
- Offered as a later invitation

Leader Reminder

Jesus never rushed transformation.
He stayed.
So should we.

Friday Evening (Arrival & Safety)

Goal: Grounding, not uncovering.

- Welcome + posture setting
- Session 1: *Meeting at the Well*
- Session 2: *Living Water*
- No tests
- No jars yet
- No pressure to share

People should leave Friday night feeling:

"I'm safe here. Nothing is being pulled out of me."

This matters more than anything.

Saturday Morning (Recognition, Not Resolution)

Goal: Awareness without digging.

- Session 3: *Truth & Identity*
- Session 4: *Worship & Deflection*
- Gentle group reflection (pattern-level only)

Important boundary:
Do **not** introduce the Surface Test first thing in the morning.

Let people *sit with the story* before they sit with themselves.

Saturday Afternoon / Evening (Naming Without Weight)

Goal: Naming patterns, not diagnosing selves.

- Session 5: *Witness & Return*
- Transition → Jars Overview
- Surface Test (with *strong* pastoral framing)

Critical facilitator language here:

"Nothing you notice today requires fixing before you leave."

No Deeper Test yet.
This protects people from emotional overload.

Sunday Morning (Release, Not Excavation)

Goal: Leave people lighter than they arrived.

Options:

- Short devotional wrap-up
- Corporate prayer
- Communion
- A quiet reading of John 4:13–14

Then this line (out loud):

Send them home **with** the Deeper Test — not *through* it.

Sunday Closing Script (Send People Home Steady)

(Read aloud — this matters)

Before we go, hear this clearly:

You do not need to finish this workbook to be faithful.

You do not need to name everything you carry today.
You do not need clarity before you leave this room.

What you noticed matters.
What stirred matters.
What you did *not* yet name also matters.

Jesus did not meet the woman at the well to give her assignments.
He met her to give her water.

Some of you may return to these pages later.
Some may sit quietly with what surfaced.
Some may realize you are not ready — and that is okay.

Living water does not flood the soul.
It rises patiently.

So go gently.
Trust what God continues.
And know this:

You are not behind.
You are not exposed.
You are not alone.

Amen.

You do not need to complete this workbook to be faithful.
What matters is what God continues after you leave.